MOSTLY CLEARING

ALSO BY MICHAEL GOTTLIEB

What We Do: Essays for Poets
I Had Every Intention
Dear All
Letters To A Middle Aged Poet
The Dust (10th anniversary edition)
Memoir And Essay
The Likes Of Us
Lost And Found
Careering Obloquy
Gorgeous Plunge
More Than All (with Ted Greenwald)
The Night Book
The River Road
Valu Pac
New York
The Blue Slope
Pantographic
96 Tears
Local Color / Eidetic Deniers

MOSTLY CLEARING

Michael Gottlieb

ROOF BOOKS
NEW YORK

ISBN: 978-1-931824-95-8
Library of Congress Control Number: 2019947954

Cover photograph by Michael Gottlieb

Author's photograph by Isabel Gottlieb

Portions of this book originally appeared in *Otoliths 51* and *Otoliths 52*, and the *Brooklyn Rail*. Thanks to the editors

NEW YORK STATE OF OPPORTUNITY | Council on the Arts This book is made possible, in part, by the New York State Council on the Arts with the support of Governor Andrew Cuomo and the New York State Legislature.

Roof Books
are published by
Segue Foundation
300 Bowery, New York, NY 10012
seguefoundation.com

Roof Books
are distributed by
Small Press Distribution
1341 Seventh Street
Berkeley, CA. 94710-1403
800-869-7553 or spdbooks.org

for Robin

CONTENTS

MOSTLY CLEARING

1

so surely

as if there could be
any doubt any longer

the realization dawns
this was
mostly tidal air

that end-of-days
as heralded by Caspar David Friedrich
—that long view across the lake
rising above that sheet of mist—
we want to say
has now run its course

now cured one and all
those diseases of despair

with the warmest of regards
you showed them
the dummy

among all that
we have been faced with today
there are some things

we are resolved
must be true

this was our life
laid out before us
a surprisingly sunny sizzle reel

in the glow
of the burnished bright-work
we made out our reflection

at the end of the day
the unavoidable realization
that we too
even us
might be counted
among the saved

doctor I can walk again!

2

towering rebuttals making way
to dizzy effrontery

the conversation's calving formations

I wish
I was the first
to think
of that

the cheerful contrivance
found in
the steerage of the compliment

an out-group
out of practice

it was a commonplace
following on
that kind of rough justice
you always ended up the better for

it was the Swinging Sixties

a compound mending
based on a learned response

leading to the well-founded premise
from which flowed
all the honeyed demarches
adorning our table talk

where we tarried
over the years

we've still got it
we've got it from here
we hold tight

don't let go

3

what settled on top of the conversation

an epochal event

what you assumed at first
was idle flattery
jimmies
scattered across
an untroubled surface
beneath which
drowsily stirred
some soon to be roused
hopes

it was a name-day
it was a famous conversion
it was the sort of assortment
you once could only dream of

it was like that special person
showed up for your reading
as if it had only been a few weeks
since you last crossed paths

and he was as alive
as you or me

4

no overegged argument
this not-unwelcome attention
no longer grudge-savvy
not anymore

as it happens
this might be of some moment

one of the principals
tossing away her objections
rises in her seat
visibly delighted

a hail of unfeigned greeting
from the bespoke affinity group
striding across this once star-crossed adventureland
a liberal serving
of sympathetic possibility

a sufficient sum
of the sterner stuff

not all that difficult
to discern in the underpainting

we notice
one has seen fit to present herself
having perhaps somehow summoned up
the requisite amount of get-up-and-go
somehow making it to the door
and so putting herself
firmly in the column
of those we still count
our once-careening cohort

in whose presence

at the end of the day
even a day
like this

bucking up
this cock-eyed catastrophist

gratefully added
to the strength of our number

5 I JUST PLAIN LIKE THE WAY YOU THINK!

what is a business day
anyway

at one in the morning
in the back of a cab
on the way
to an unfamiliar address
near Herald Square

we told ourselves
no interest
no conflict
that was a joke

at first
a thinly settled truth

to slip and fall in love

through the mountains
this beckoning passage
this gleaming lowland
we hoped to espy

it itself
we fancied

somehow fashioned
from the half light

a regnant reality
a go/no-go
a pursuit plane

as if
sending up a flare

hand to hand
in the canteen

for our part
climbing that cloud staircase
not too summery
not too much lift
not too much glare
not all that much to bear
not too easeful
not too matchy
none too soon

on the back foot no longer
even according to this
fallen world view

signing at all the
indicated places

resolutely resolving
to remain
faithful to the archive

the range officers
beckoning to us

I was
more than enough
of a trial
for the two of us

lucky for me
you were both
judge and jury

this coastal route

this embowered byway
altogether untrodden
on my way
to find you

6 THE TAPE-RECORDING ANGEL

in the bonus room

a return on dicey
demonstrated by
the steeply raked curve
where the general anti-declinist
finds a new alloy to anneal

the optimistic spirit level
resolves our doubts
a tiny bobbing vessel

one who never met a recourse note
he didn't like

your Instamatic
your Super 8
where are they now

an unsporting surge
a not-uncaring surmise
and an inspiring use case
walk into a bar

a spur of stubborn agency
noted by
the tape-recording angel

7 BEFORE WE BEGIN

now put down your pencils

this simple trick
will save you
from the fires
of eternal damnation

the rough sleepers
the rained-on estate
the grayed-out cement
the pebbledash

the once-ignored
no longer in their proper place
thankfully

where the lush workers and night walkers
repaired for a quick pick me up
where our kind
felt most at home

so much better than
a face-plow from the loge

the once ebullient name calling
the combed and curried

the carefully lit alcove
the token of esteem

there was rampant cross selling
a kind of happily suborned subtext
sort of like passing the hat

this particular brand of white-out
this so-called world entire

what we have come
to expect of you

just the beginning
of what must be acknowledged

you know of course
we too walked
these same streets
in our youth

that all too often under-appreciated asset
abandon

which so often
dissolved
in the tumbler

what it meant
to have a rent party

when from the first
you evinced a keen
and robust interest
in all things that weren't
your business

summiting at the top of mind

which is part of your piquant charm

what makes this
truly a minimal viable product

where we were often to be found

when it came time to do
that victory lap dance

what we want you
—you who are on the road—
to know

it really was
a walk in the park

this newfound gloaming
this once fugitive fondness
this dogged commitment to optimism

this is what we summon up
this is why
you are here

this is the rank order
of our hopes for you

a near run thing
a benign reign
a vase upon the table
a busy palette knife

it was for you
all that toil
every wearying year

and away we go

this far
we can accompany you

read this silently
while I read this aloud

8

I got this hat
at the
tractor
logico-philosophicus
supply company

9 THAT'S ALL FOLKS

even
the great malingerer
he too
coming to evince
that well-founded fear
of word finding

that immortal episode

momentarily speechless

eventually
yanking on Elmer's hat
with both hands

"flaps down
Doc!"

what spurt of productivity
what disproof of concept
what song on our lips

he was a trickster
and so
we fancied ourselves similarly

it's purpose built
it's a curing system
it's like opening a ticket

how we tabulate
the table set before us
the carriage return
the omnibus
the repurposed enclosure
the point of service
in the break down lane
the tip of tailings
towering over the settlement

"I wonder what the poor rabbits are doing this season"

the hoary ordinance
on the books still
the prefigured
the as of right
the set asides

the matted fur

decades later
now we own it

we too
among the committed

10

telling ourselves
and each other
this indeed leads nowhere else
but to that irreducible eventuality

as if starting out
there we could be found
at a sagging beaux-arts pile
in an old spa town
among some half-forgotten foothills

holding high
that bunch of grapes
bronzed
starting to oxidize

they have feelings
too
don't they

we agreed
this is what we need
once and for all
one neck to choke

what did we know

11

durable goods
real and true

we were all
medium well

once and done

those parts
of our better selves
which now and then
need to be taken out
and aired

an ark for our feelings
an immortal ferry service

the best and highest use
of our time

12 IS IT GOOD FOR THE POETS

tearing through the countryside
a divining-rod by our side

what I'm hearing

that indubitable assurance
a kind of bounded conversation
"you'll be just fine"

the celebratory tolling
the resplendent resource room
that darn informal economy

entirely in keeping
a kind of piece work

a surfeit of cirro cumulous
swanning down the boulevard

we came upon
the scene
as if
in a dream

under
the big tent

tent cards
inscribed with our real names

an averral
a mess set
a kinetic operation

kitted out for a cotillion

landing on someone's last nerve

a daily special

13

who knew
who talked
someone must

that dead man's curve
where once
we spun out

perchance to persevere

to wait no longer

what its really like

thus
I refute you
house of tears

"it shall be the study of our life to make you happy"

if not who
if not when
if not here
if not us

14 GIVE THE PEOPLE WHAT THEY WANT

in the copse
blooming solitary
a simple woodland flower

if you wish

who made good
who made bad

we touched you up a bit
everyone agreed
it was a welcome improvement

this secret codicil
this rain of compliments

the way
subtraction can
grow on you
on us, on all of us

a frank crowd pleaser
evergreen
a never fail
what at first
you were sure

was nothing less than
an unredeemable dud
now your most requested

knowing the value
of a dollar

an inarguable

your game chorines
your sunny chore boys
like multitudes appearing
one spring morning
encamped in our midst
a gentle waving army
upon the hillside

your unflinching portrayal

this afternoon's
honeyed practiced line

you saw a strong family resemblance
you had an unquenched thirst for conformation
you thought you knew what became of us

if this be a frank profession

a chapter in every city
a recording secretary
a welcome wagon

we are all in league with you

we want to say
feel free
to stop by
any old time

it's not a final sale

these are the things
we always wanted you to know

we will go your surety

this is the central holding

15 ROLL ON MIGHTY LINE

a silent alarm
a restless district

any one of us
the kind of driver
for whom
green meant go
and yellow meant
go faster

a decision tree
loaded down with the fruit
of our hopes

how they survived
in this world

an ideé fixe like
supply chain or procurement

famously unprepared

once and for all

always accounting
in arrears

to be young
in a time like this

the poet's life
so devil-may-care
and happy-go-lucky
that's the one for me

you want to reply
that you can't count cards
if you can't count

to profess
to abjure
an act of contrition

all the arguments
that spilled from that stuffed file
that served to militate for
that great-man theory
of poetry

at the head
of that particular pack
of lies

we cast it all down!

16

what did
we have
to lose

what night terrors
gave way to

a backsplash
for our tears

channeling
all those
incautious effusions

'spray and pray'
for so long
more than enough

what we wanted
before we knew it

the vain attempt
studies itself
in the rear-view mirror

he was the spitting image
wiped from the corner
of her mouth

these were all
fighting words

17

what it means
to say
you know
of course
this means war
with a Bronx accent

18

suddenly
during the so-called proffer session
a big fat one
right in the kisser!

dodging the careening catafalque

in the field
behind the barred gate
like a ghost
long lain there
he arose from his place

to come out with it
to slip the surly bonds
and make a break for it
to rip off the gauze
to ask each attendee
to step up to the dais
and say a few words
about him

it was a fully loaded brush
it was the business end of his proposition

he retained all his faculties
it's just that some of them
were on sabbatical

not unsurprisingly
everyone agreed
this was a good look
for him

for so long
we assumed
he was made
of toner

the toll
upon him
all those years

mother of mercy
is this end
of poor Rico?

the weight of all that finery
like so much cordage

the regalia of the inevitable

19

landing nearby
another
artlessly unaffected
schematic

a surprisingly tuneful
retort

whereas

willingly he submits
to your caresses

a foundational messaging
this destiny belief
inscribed upon each brow

it all eventually
is meant
to come out
in the wash

you too
look good
in white

a kind of summons
for us all

I really liked the cut of your jib

this call and response
may be monitored

20 DISAMBIGUATION WINS BY A NOSE

"it's better than pie!"

everything must go
if I say so myself

a kind of day camp
for a tranche
that always had trouble
doing the math

threading together
those fugitive lanyards

it was manifest

where he was sure
he belonged
in his eyes
the way he held his head
a kind of fixed address

this distance qualifier
this shield phrase

a formerly irresolute
affirmation

at one time
content
to vote present

there are some things
we must evidently abjure
if we want
to face you
—you who are arriving later—
in the end

withal and within

the faintly luminous
fold of ridge
the front of the valley

grander than

altogether

disambiguation
wins
by a nose

21

a pass / fail

who can it be
who's never
occasionally
found wanting

taking this
as it comes

we had to bend down
to make out
the almost inaudible sigh

who used to
teach to the test

as is our due
we pace
the streets
unrecognized

we wanted some
it didn't matter
that it's a cereal

we called it
Lust for Life

22 AN EYE-WATERING OPPORTUNITY

look smart

eyes right

we always thought
the question
was properly put

convincing ourselves
how much darker
it would soon grow
was always
so heartening

it's not your fault
it never was

everyone
doesn't
have to take
their medicine

23

seated at a help desk
for the helpless

keeping the line open

abiding despite
daunting odds

they still apply
all the hoary admonitions
the incommensurately obdurate
those gems of misattribution

this
we hold close

that fondly
recalled breakfast

that unswerving belief
in untimely ends

"I miss
miss
you
dearly"

24 THE SEMI-PERMANENT FIRMAMENT

it was just
those g-forces again
pooling
at our ankles

I thought
I saw
something
in you

this new notational system

no longer cut
on the conformation bias

if you can believe it

those beginnings
how we went about
living our lives
pretending there was
no duty of care

how lucky
are we

still
putting one
variable foot
in front
of another

25

as if this
was something
we should ever
have to
have been
taught

26 LACHRYMOSE-INTOLERANT

the weight of the years
may try to hold you up

an unusual aversion

handling those princely sums

"they have decided
to go
in a different direction"

it sometimes
comes to this

for decades
a mis-heard
grain of refrain
one day
for some reason
you hear aright
for the first time

it is as if
we have all
suddenly become
lachrymose-intolerant

27

not just
a petty criminal
superficial too

jostling for a better view

restless and eager

a weekend pass
getting to yes

the poets'
vise-like grip
on that market

there for the picking

our means and methods
lie close to the surface

anyone so inclined
can make them theirs

what
we are obliged
always to ask

are we
fit for purpose

where
we are prompted
to say…

it was good to see you

we'll wait here

I think
you should
have that
looked at

28 YOUR NEXT AND FINAL STOP

don't forget to check
the overhead bin

what must needs
be attended to

signals
are flashing

the belongings
you arrived with

the maintenance of way

contents
may settle
during shipping

thanks for stopping by

29

their motto
doing less
with more

in the land
of the free
association
a kind of
gestural spectatoring

a punch list
for the
punch drunk

the fancy dress
donned by
the fun-loving
occupants

you want
to say yes

your eyes
are windows
pull down
the shades

eventually
we all need become
adepts

and toggle between
perdition
and
Pernell Roberts

a pillbox
a recurring charge
a bonus room
a dunking
a sole provider

to wit

this
pretty pass

I watch you
rise above

30

it simply
can't be beat

I remember
your apgar

becoming
what
we hold
most dear

breathy
incorrigible
irrepressible

I embarrass you
that's my job

I took
your picture
do you
want it
back

I hold this
in my hand
we called it
a transparency

31

JMW Turner
wert that thou
were breathing today
to see this morn’s dawn
over the closed up K Mart

32

a sort of trade show
of the mooted

why we seek repetition
what erudition
can never solve for

a hastily-converted
high school gym

the reason
we really get up
in the morning

to all appearances
a now-placid estuary

a storyboard test
where those fears
may be
once and for all
summarily dismissed

the youth league

overcoming
a sorry childhood

the ragged colors
nailed to the mast

no longer
missing my
cargo cult

I walk
freely among you

witting
for once

this is just what
the trailer promised

it's always
4:03
somewhere

the happy day
when the irregulars
reached our town

33

I remember
fun city

what takes the cake

plush toys
for the grown ups

what we tried
to bury
in the conversation pit

task lighting
for the idle

the difference
between namesake
and eponymous

this I bequeath you

34

irked by joy

misrule's
residual
process-flow

a laugh most dulcet

only
our due

this end up

why we've been sent here

the orders
are under seal

it is not ours
even if
we're the only ones
who care

an article of faith
that words can save us

in this language
we trust

35 OTHERWISE IT WOULD BE FOLLY

we had words
for lunch

maybe the best disinfectant
sunlight
not the best deodorant

twice removed

that's not nothing

a good assist

our stated purpose

the reserves are mobilized

what we were socialized
to recognize as
nothing more than animal spirits
evergreen
ascendant
irrepressible

have the times really changed

seeking to stake
their knowledge claims
the successors-in-interest

if we came across them
today
what would we call them

those unities
of time
place
and action

a life sentence
with some noun phrases

why did it take so long
to see them
for what
they are

36 A CLAIM-RACE

see it
name it
pocket it

everyone should have
at least
one

but then
I set you free
little word

deeply unserious
and so
all the more revered

a man
a plan
a Canaletto

as this latest thing
a magic marker
cast its spell
upon us

37

of a morning

now that you mention it

what possibly
could fall
out of this
clear blue sky

a dagwood sandwich
a not unwelcome anvil
a bank error in your favor
a burnished apple
a long-lost friend

— almost anything!

38 SHELLY'S GREAT WHEEL

we pass along
the fiery road

a kind of set list
stapled to the articles of faith

the green shoots too

a salubrious uptick

a scenic overlook
an unspooling hinterland

a push-in of hopefulness

pouring us
into these casts

warming snaps

we know
if there is no deposit
maybe
there is no return

not heedless
but regardless

39

the unexamined life
upon further examination
was looking
better and better

one door down
from defeat

for both
mailing and shipping

our address
for so long

but then one day

glazed with rain

trailed by
some fowl
of some sort

the movers arrived

with their great red wheelbarrow!

40 THE VENERABLE ALFRED E NEUMAN'S BEATIFIC RICTUS

all it should take
to die
a happy man!

there's so much
to like
about this
where do I start

this sad sack simulacrum of a sorting regime

this is what used to be buried in the basement

this child's portion
this sales motion
this unreserved gauge
this artful display of precedence
as if there was
all the time in the world

this rumble
of armored vehicles
maneuvering on the approaches

gathered at the waist
of the conversation

that is not to say
that we do not all
crave what we construe
our due

for our upright ambitions
a kind of starry flyway

cause enough

what we long pretended
wishfulness could win us

what we all
never quite lost
that hankering for
this fresh starter's gun
this land of second-chances
this great room
this self-guided tour
this attempt at tempering
this uncanny likeness
this declined vial

all the swooning certainty of youth

where we knew
we were always
meant to end up

where once it sprouted in all directions

as if we really
ever knew what we were about
as if you could pretend
you didn't notice
as if being mistaken
for another poet
was so terrible
as if this
was really your fate
as if you really thought
you didn't make a difference

don't be afraid
to ask
for what
you're sure
you don't deserve

41 FEATS OF ARMS

tonight
while we speak
from a moonless sky
men are dropping
onto France

the mantle of hills
the practiced vanishing point

me
along with the rest
agape

looking upon
those frozen eddies

beholding
the incommensurable
strung like beads

the signature effect

which is
to be clear

I didn't know what to say

I was a hired hand
if you will

I wanted to be the architect
of all this glad
ruin

issuing my own paper

a boom service

don't you
wonder why
I'm always so glad
to see you

I wanted to believe
I didn't really need
all that chrome

what these disparate
wants
all have in common

what I found
in myself

discovered in a box-lot
a keepsake

showing me
the lay of the land

a theater of operations
a kind of assay office
presided over by
an end stage door Johnny

what the market
did so well

my naked asseveration
balled up
like a fist

even for me
all of this
might otherwise
have seemed
a bit on the nose
or a sop to my self regard

like a press gang
of my peers

it was by design
it was quite the night
it was arrayed for me
rolling hills and dales

all picked out
by the occasional comet
arcing across a winking valley

put me in
coach
I'm ready

42 AVAST MATEYS

another rower
in this galley

blithely stirring
the solution

chained to all that

a simple syrup

the indeterminate clause
the ever-thorny subject

inducing a reagent

as if
back then
we were
making deposits
at a fog bank

the once inexorable

against present value

what we keep coming back to

not forgot
never gone

43

to be so lucky

to grow old enough
to some day
be surprised
by this

what I now feel obliged to stipulate to

what you always saw through

those blessed
impure thoughts

after all these years
admitting

no longer
a stranger to
this emotion

like a lifer
miraculously
sprung from
solitary

how much I need you

that object-permanence
so devotedly wished for
turning it over in your hand

ask
a woman
who knows

for so long
starring
in my own biopic

usually
we put this
over there
and there
it stays

with that part of me
which you gave back
to me

I try it on for size
if it doesn't fit now
maybe
I will grow into it

44

newly arrived
at our shores
the king tide

at flood stage finally

that course of doubt
crashes collapsing
upon its own weight

we are free!

in our lifetime
the once stigmatized behavior

a business model
back then
contingent upon
chucking people over the gunwales

you are better than that

the unchaperoned concepts
now free to mingle

at ease

as you were
as we used to say
let your fingers

do the walking

all good hosts
know
you can never
have enough
mixer

45 PRIMA FACIE PLAUSIBLE

I know
you are
but what am I!

the old painter
who says
interesting
if true

the boxer who says
I'm ok
you're ko'd

the guy
who tells us
I found
my love
in the lost luggage

the once mandatory
two-key launch protocol

transfixed by

this carefree-for-all
this happy scrum

this color thankfully
never found in nature

this cheerful disarray

the value leader
the field justice
in an unplowed field

act your age
not your shoe size

that whopping differential

46 I WILL GLADLY

I will gladly
pay you
wednesday
for a hamburger
today
and I promise
to come to
your reading
on saturday

47 WE WERE ALL ONCE OF FIGHTING AGE

the grounded aircraft
in the breezeway

the unquiet night

bedeviled
by the follow-on shades

the poets past

those who are gone
or should be

by thoughts of them
those who didn't make it
or couldn't take it
we are possessed
naturally

a youth spent
too close
to the speakers

then the roaring seas

from which
so many
never return

those terrible latitudes
the infernal forties

does it seem
so long ago

but who is not spoken for

still occasionally
caught sight of
scrabbling down
soiled sidewalks

a harmless eccentric
describing a curve
what was once called
a wizened crone
an old cove
a lovable barmy

we were all once
of fighting age

someone says
you can eat well
or sleep well
just not both

48 WHERE THE POETS TAKE THE WATERS

where the poets
take the waters

asking nicely
for a fight

the blasé settee
the 'doofus' stand-in
the equivalent of a mere needle-stick
the dry goods

I can't imagine
anywhere I'd rather be
tonight

what we all naturally
have a hankering for
such blithe assurance

your rod
and your staff
they comfort me

without apparent volition

they ring down from
the look-out

the sally-gate
the happy accident
the cracking mask of resolve

what is laid on
with a trowel

among the plantings
the towering folly

all the things
you don't need
to be ashamed of
anymore

standing at what we assumed
was a safe distance

surveying
the so-called love-nest

it was finally clear
even to intelligences
such as ours

of a piece

price
unconscious

drawn easily
on this topic

what inevitably takes
a lifetime
to master

what is our highest calling

an untenanted allotment
to which we bring
our joint and several fortunes

a current coursing through the crowd

a caravanserai for our hopes

a victory
at sea

everyone has
the goods
on us

in the lighting district
the gift district
the notions district

where we learned
free verse
isn't free

doing business in the beating heart of the city

under our own buttonwood tree
this is our practice
the pitch where we fetch up
making our markets

AFTERWORD: HOW I CAME TO WRITE CERTAIN OF THESE LINES

1 ASHBERY, DEAD

Ashbery was dead. This was around the time that I began work on this poem. John Ashbery, dead. I had last seen him at a Christmas party. How long ago had it been? A year ago? Two? It was at a big house in the country. He sat in a side parlor while the poets who were in attendance collected there and gathered by his side. We would go and get drinks and chat with the other guests, then come back and sit with him some more.

When I heard the news, I went to my shelves and pulled down his books and laid them on my desk.

Not long after, I was asked to participate in a memorial reading for him. We each took turns, first reading, then telling a story about him. My story was about attending a dinner in the Village after a reading he gave at the Ear Inn, at some restaurant on MacDougal. I'm sure it was the first time we met. Why did we end up there, blocks and blocks from the reading? Was there nowhere closer to eat, even back then? As I recall, everyone at the dinner was a guy. There were maybe six of us. I remember there was easy, flowing conversation.

2 RE-READING HIM

Those books on my desk, books I hadn't opened in years, as the weeks and months passed I found myself returning to them: *Three Poems, The Tennis Court Oath*—early books, old books, worn paperback books. As I reread them, I found myself struck, more than struck, bowled over, by one quality, one particular, salient attribute. How had I not noticed it when reading him the first time? How was it that none of the tributes to him appearing now mentioned this?

It was there on every page, irresistible, irrepressible: an effervescent, jaunty, Fifties, often-jokey, Pop-ish optimism.

All those French quotes, every image from Hollywood, the soda pop brands, the billboard images, the quotes which could have been snatched from a Lichtenstein painting—'Oh, Brad!'—it was ever-present; a happy, funny optimistic thread that ran through every page.

3 THEN, RE-READING THE NEW YORK POETS… AND WHY WE STOPPED READING THEM WHEN WE DID

Over the following weeks I opened up other books I hadn't looked at in years. I found myself rereading his friends: Schuyler, Koch and—perhaps coincidentally, since I'd just picked up his biography—O'Hara as well, another great looming presence. And, although I can't say I never thought about those guys, though, of course, they weren't all guys, and they weren't all white either, for that matter, the fact is, I hadn't sat down and read, really read them, in a long time. Now, I saw that bright, gleaming, redolent, vibrant optimism in them too.

Where did that optimism come from? It was the Fifties—that accounted for some of it. We Americans were victors, weren't we? We'd vanquished our foes in the war just ended. And, despite the hate and fear spread by McCarthy and the likes of him, we flourished—or a good number of us did—in the flush of post-war boom.

Optimism: it certainly wasn't and isn't everything that is big and important and true about O'Hara, Koch and Ashbery, but for some reason, in the Fall of 2017, it all struck me with terrific force, decades after I bought those books.

Rereading them also summoned up certain memories. I had studied poetry and writing in college and my copy of Ron Padgett's and David Shapiro's New York School anthology dates to then. I'm holding it right now, thumbing through it, coming across Brainard's lovely drawings, and there, on the flyleaf, a surprise—my signature as a nineteen-year-old, in blue ballpoint, ridiculously awkward, a child's hand.

Back then, the poets who were represented in that anthology were, along with guys like Olson and Creeley, the most radical, out-there poets I was exposed to. And the fact is, they weren't really taken very seriously by my teachers. In those years the literature faculty at Bennington, when it came to their joint and several points-of-view on many topics, seemed in many ways a far-flung satrapy of the English Department at Yale and when it came to contemporary poets, they largely plumped for people like Merwin and Merrill and A.R. Ammons.

I've already written about some of these memories: coming to New York after college, hanging out at the Gotham Book Mart, meeting life-long friends for the first time. Some I haven't written about: discovering the Phoenix Book Shop, going to the Poetry Project for the first time. And, as I sit here, holding that anthology in my hand, suddenly remembering: one night, with Alan Davies, a year or two after he and I met... going to visit Joe Brainard. Joe in a dark crew-necked sweater, small and neat.

Some of the memories, written about or not, were about arguments and debates that took place decades ago. As Language poetry came to define itself, we started identifying poets that we could, or wanted to claim descent from. Those exemplars from college were out. That was fine with me, I'd rejected them myself. Black Mountain and the Objectivists were in, obviously. And, when it came to the New York School, with the notable exception of Ashbery, well, most of them were Out.

The direct inheritors of the New York School were the St. Marks poets and we were sure they didn't really like us. They said all we did was write theory and criticism, which was so terribly unfair, wasn't it? All that was so very long ago but, no doubt, it was around then, by and large, I stopped reading those New York School guys, with the exception of Ashbery. He was different. We could say he was one of us.

4 THE NEW YORK THEY WROTE ABOUT... THE SAME ONE I GREW UP IN

I had also forgotten what consummate, inveterate New Yorkers these New York poets were. New York is there, in poem after poem of theirs, a New York that was half-familiar—the New York of the Fifties. A New York of smoky clubs and steam rising in columns from early morning avenues. It was the same New York I caught sight of as a child from the suburbs: a New York of automats, of subways with cane seats, of black and green and white police cars, of grand movie palaces I was taken to once a year and the old Yankee Stadium with its subway girder columns and its immaculate emerald outfield. It was a New York before air conditioning, filled with men in fedoras and women in nylons.

It was this New York: overawing me every visit, holding my mother's hand, emerging from the dark train platform into Grand Central's vast echoing concourse, thronged with racing hordes of men in suits. Each time dazzled by Kodak's huge Colorama sign taking up the entire eastern end—where the Apple store sits now—that giant transparency and its glowing scenes of suburban serendipity. All those staged Kodachrome snaps of cook-outs and skating parties and families gathered over TV dinners. It all looked like just where I lived, how I lived. It was uncanny.

It was this New York: walking down Fifth Avenue, holding her hand, on our way to Orbach's, after a lunch at Schrafft's. I caught sight of a plainly dressed old woman with a briefcase, briskly striding alone, uptown, towards us, other passersby making way for her. A kind of nimbus around her, that's how I remember it now, like Siddhartha pacing through his village. People just knew that amongst them walked this special being. My mother bending down to whisper, "that's Eleanor Roosevelt..."

As I reread those poets now, I asked myself how much of their impact on me then, when I first read them, and how much of this sudden swooning for them now, was due to their effortless summoning of that New York? And, how much of my identity as a New York poet, for that is certainly how I describe myself, is the fruit of seeds they planted?

5 DECIDING TO FOCUS ON OPTIMISM… AND MY THREE OTHER LONG-STANDING FOCUS AREAS

How could I have been so unaware, so clueless, for so long? It was there on every page. As I reread those poets now—now, in these dark times, when every day it seems like things couldn't get worse, then promptly did, and then the next day got worse still—there it was, that refreshing optimism, I found myself thirsty for it. For the first time since I began publishing, as I now read and reread Ashbery and the others, I sat down and decided, constructively, that this work, this new poem I had just started, was going to be about *something*. It was going to have a theme: this optimism.

I wanted, I needed, I decided, to capture it, or try.

The only other time I decided upon a theme, in that declarative kind of way, was immediately after 9/11, when, like every other poet in New York, I sat down and wrote a poem. Mine is called *The Dust*. And that, I think, was different. None of us had a choice. Back then, we had to sit down and write.

So, why now? Why this poem? Because I felt invested. Ashbery's optimism, all of their optimism, it filled me up. And all of a sudden it became clear—we need this. Now.

As I worked on this poem and sought to imbue it with those attributes which I found in Ashbery and the others, I also found myself looking back what I had published over the years in a new light.

Even though my friends and I, in our youth, were poets who had decisively declared that subject matter was obsolete and irrelevant, it had become clear over the years, that we too, like everyone else, were writing about *something*. And the something that had bubbled up in my work over the years... was what? Well, as I've come to say: I have three subjects:

First, there is the life of the poet, the question of how we, as poets, live our lives, or don't. How do we connect with each other? How are we a community? What responsibility do we have to each other, and ourselves? How does the way we act towards each other, and ourselves, reflect our values, as poets?

When we go out to the world with what we've written—what then? That the world doesn't give a toss for us, for what we do, but that we go on doing it anyway, partly for our own sakes, partly for each other, but also because we believe that the world needs us, even as it ignores or belittles us—because what would a world without poets be—what does that say about us? This is a topic I've returned to over and over.

Second, there is New York. Not just the New York of my childhood, but the New York that is the sum of all its pasts, and its gorgeous and heartless present, as well as its entirely uncertain future. There is the fabulously fading seat of empire I decanted into as a young poet in the Seventies, beneath its shopworn patina the endlessly multitudinous entrepôt it always was, but has now metastasized from, almost out of all recognition, as it has come to abandon all but one of its longstanding roles, that being a coaling station for the world's richest and most criminal. That is here too.

Third, there is language itself. Even early on I felt that among the Language poets there weren't many others who were specifically possessed by, consumed by language itself like I was—that is to say, *vocabulary, words*. Not sentences, or the sentence, but words themselves.

The power of words, on their own, unfettered by formal grammar or conventional prosody, much less the dead hand of subject matter, the force of words, by themselves, perhaps thrown together by chance or other combination seemed all-powerful. These were words that arrived from every corner of the language—served up by the city in a way that only New York could—non-literary words, words from the worlds of business and crime, from the city's streets and from its signage, the conversation of cabbies and cops, along with ridiculous faded literary language thrown in for contrast, all of that combined to foment meaning on a scale I could not have guessed that afternoon I sat down, after reading Clark Coolidge the first time, upon discovering a book of his at the Gotham Book Mart, and I realized I could pull all of that language into poems, because Clark showed me a way. That was the day my life changed as a poet.

However, while looking at words that way became part and parcel of my project, might there have been other factors at play? Now I wonder to what degree the approach I adopted—removing words from their traditional context—was related to the isolation I felt as a writer as the years wore on.

Similarly, when it comes to the approaches to diction and word choice I've developed over the years, in addition to the words gleaned from the sources listed above, there were other words, arcane five-dollar-words, *squamos, iatrogenic, architrave, intervallic,* that I inserted into poems. I told myself they were gorgeous, baubled things with fantastic mouth-feel, that their relative inscrutability put the rest of each poem's vocabulary into higher relief. Now I wonder if there was something else going on. Was I wheeling up that kind of artillery so I would seem serious?

While I've in the last few years tried to rein in that impulse, perhaps it's no different than another habit—one I am no way close to being able to address: those pauses I put into my speech, along with that surely-annoying habit of stopping sentences and starting them over… to make them better-worded, to say it—whatever it is—using just the right words.

Also, looking back over the years, I believe I can see something else seeping in. Maybe it didn't appear until I was in my thirties or forties, surfacing often in the adjectives, adding a flavor, an often self-conscious, perhaps self-regarding sentiment; a not un-grim, dystopian, perhaps depressed, point of view: things are bad, and they are only going to get worse.

And *that*—that is what I decided as I sat with Ashbery's books on my desk, as I began work on this book—I was going to replace in this new poem.

I decided that I was going to go from "ailing dioramas"—a phrase that appeared in a book of mine from the Eighties, brought to the world by the same publisher as this book—to "sunny disposish" in this one.

6 HOW, BY SUMMONING THOSE POETS' OPTIMISM, THEIR STYLINGS GOT PULLED AS WELL

But there's more. After I made that affirmative decision to incorporate into this poem that optimism that I saw in Ashbery and Koch and O'Hara, and in the New York School Anthology, and I began work on this book, I noticed that other qualities I associate with them appeared also, unbidden, of their own accord. Purposely easy word play, simple, direct, emotional appeals, frank addresses to my wife, and to my children and my friends and younger poets. Not to mention imagery from my childhood—bits of cartoons and television shows and movies—corresponding, I suppose, to the pop imagery that we associate with those poets, and the artists I associate with them—Lichtenstein and Rosenquist and the rest, and of course, Brainard too.

And when it came to those direct, frank emotional addresses, I was surprised by how easily they rose up out of me. I told myself at first that they were just another kind of talk-track, another kind of vocabulary, just another specialist diction of the sort I'd been importing into my poetry for a long time—like the scientific or legal or business jargon or snatches of NYC street signage that had forever appeared there. 'Self' words are no different than 'social' words—that's what I told myself. Ashbery and other others gave me permission, as it were, to write like this. But once I began, I realized that there were things I really wanted to say. Is that so wrong? For a Language poet… maybe. Is this a sign of something? Of aging? Of impending something-or-other? Crumbling standards, creeping decrepitude? I'm not sure. But I proceeded, I kept on.

Like everyone else, I suspect, I have a band of little folk in my head—ideal readers, theoretical readers, actual readers, readers living and dead, perhaps unborn—who react to what I'm writing as I write it. Sometimes I think of them as internal editors. Sometimes I suspect they're censors. Sometimes I need to silence them. At least I try. God knows what they'll think of all this.

7 SO…

But I want to say that, now that I've finished this book, the optimism that I felt I need to incorporate into these pages is not some foreign body, not some exotic or some invasive… now it's something that I believe, despite what faces me, a man, a straight white man, at this time of his life, despite what faces us all when we get up in the morning, despite the news we read every day, despite all.

And, is it optimism or is it hope? I think it's optimism—because I don't hope that things are going to get better—I expect them to. There is something inside me now, somehow Ashbery and the others put it there: things are going to get better. It makes me confident that we will eventually look back at these times and shake our heads, marveling at first, that things did indeed manage to get better. And then eventually we will look back, though I'm not sure exactly when, and it will all seem to have been somehow inevitable. Of course, there were dark days, we'll say. But of course, it got better, it *had* to.

Perhaps I am different now. I do think things do just get better, as times goes on. Maybe they have to get worse first, before they get better, and certainly it is not clear how bad they'll have to get first, or for how long, but better days are surely ahead. I also believe it has to do with the country we live in. This country, despite everything, despite all the fear and lies and hate, and the blood and destruction it was built upon, and all that has been done and continues to be done in our name, is clearly capable of getting better. It has again and again. I believe it will once more, perhaps quite soon.

I am also optimistic because we are all still writing, and I know how much we are needed, and how much what we create is needed. And how many of us there are: doing good work, making a difference—despite how useless we think we may be—making a difference in this world, in this country. What kind of world would this be, what kind of country would this be, without any poets?

And, of course, it wasn't just Ashbery's optimism that bowled me over that day, the day after he died, there was also his effervescent, irreverent joy.

One symbol, as it were, summons up all that: when it comes to Ashbery, there's one part of speech, one punctuation mark in fact, that I most associate with him. It serves up everything glad, gaily rude, brash, exciting, pop and effervescent and optimistic and joyful about him, the exclamation mark, that: !

Do I really believe all this or am I just borrowing this optimism? I'm not sure or, perhaps, the better answer is: maybe it's for you to decide. But maybe its bears mentioning, for what it's worth, that there are eleven exclamation points in this work. And that's eleven more than I've ever written before.